D1012574

Single
& Human

Ada Lum

InterVarsity Press
Downers Grove
Illinois 60515

Fourth printing, July 1979
© 1976 by Inter-Varsity
Christian Fellowship of the United
States of America

InterVarsity Press is the book-publishing
division of Inter-Varsity
Christian Fellowship, a student movement
active on campus at hundreds of
universities, colleges and schools of
nursing. For information about local
and regional activities, write IVCF,
233 Langdon St., Madison, WI 53703.

Distributed in Canada through InterVarsity
Press, 1875 Leslie St., Unit 10,
Don Mills, Ontario, M3B 2M5, Canada.

ISBN 0-87784-361-9
Library of Congress Catalog
Card Number: 75-44625

Printed in the United States of America

CONTENTS

Preface

Single and Human *began as a chapter in a book on sex and marriage called* Lovers for Life, *published in Singapore. Then it became the booklet* Quiet Plans of Love. *People have referred to that booklet title, both seriously and humorously, as* "Quiet Plans for Love," "Quiet Places for Love," "Plans for Love," "No Plans for Love," "Quick Plans for Love," "Quiet Love," "Plain Love" *and* "Whatchama-callitabout Love."

When the publishers asked me to expand the booklet into a full-sized book, I seriously considered the many helpful suggestions friends had enthusiastically made. I was intrigued that many of them were from married people. That's because they themselves are earnestly seeking to relate to their single friends.

Here are some of their suggestions. A Canadian student worker: "Give more specific examples of how to relieve sex tensions as a single woman." *An American writer:* "Expand the section on how to meet the problems." *A Latin American theologian:* "Add a chapter on the single woman's change of life." *A Singaporean bachelor:* "I have a bone to pick with you. What do you mean by saying that the male remnant in the churches often has little appeal to the girls?" *An English lady:* "Please say something about how singles can relate to married people and more about how marrieds can help singles and about how ridiculous it is for older women to try to act and look young." *A Chinese graduate student:* "Shouldn't you say something about the growing problem of bed-hopping among Christian girls? I can give you some data."

I must admit I'm terribly pleased that people have responded so to the original booklet. I have also been deeply touched by the honesty of the many people who have shared their problems through letters. If this book helps to open up the subject between singles and singles, and between singles and marrieds, I thank God. I rejoice. Let's talk about this subject more openly, more sensitively, more realistically—more biblically.

To the present edition I have added two chapters which have come home to me with increasing fascination. One is on growing older as a single woman and the other is on the human manhood of Jesus Christ.

THE GROWING SINGLES SOCIETY

1

Why aren't you married?" I am asked the question less as the years go by! But some time ago I complained to our pastor that I wished friends would stop asking it. With a twinkle in his eye he replied, "When they do, *then* you'll start worrying."

We single women have developed some answers to that question. Like, "Oh, but I'm getting married on the first."

"Wonderful! The first of what?"

"The first chance I get."

Or when others have matronizingly tried to comfort us with the possibility that "some day you'll meet the right man," the answer is, "I've met him already. I knew he was the right man. Unfortunately he didn't realize it."

Redemptive Humor

Let me assure you that my philosophy of the single life is not laughing one's way through celibacy. However, any Christian philosophy of life must include redemptive humor. It is not making light of something serious and sacred. True humor, as Jesus himself demonstrated especially in the Sermon on the Mount and certain parables, helps us to see with sudden, relieving insight another side of the reality we are considering.

Humor is one of God's gifts to us in an otherwise grim and unbearable world. Without humor we become unbalanced. We're unable to see the ludicrous in a human situation. We become either too serious about ourselves or cynical and fearful about life. Many unmarried people remain unhappy because they have not developed this perspective of redemptive humor. They see their problems only as harsh and unsolvable.

The Lessening Stigma

One positive effect of the modern women's liberation movement has been to help lessen the traditional stigma on the single woman. In fact, in America singleness in general has recently gained a certain respectability. Newspapers and magazines constantly feature articles on the apparently distinctive lifestyle of the singles. I was with a group of unmarried friends in an Asian city when a popular American magazine came out with an attractive cover for its leading article, "A New Sub-Culture: The Single Society." One of the spinsters, as they're called there, wryly commented, "It's not only in America. Look at us!"

How true. Today in nearly any modernized city around the world we find more and more single men and women, growing in numbers and developing their own nontraditional lifestyle. What factors have spawned this new society even in the Third World? Broader education, greater personal freedom and social permissiveness, more varied careers, financial independence, cosmopolitan contacts and travel, mass media—these are encouraging young people at least to postpone marriage. And not to be disregarded in some conservative societies is the fast disappearance of family-arranged marriages.

Nevertheless, society and some of our best friends can still be insensitive or embarrassed about the single adult as a fellow human being, as though he or she were a second-rate inhabitant of their earth. Moreover, even the sum total of all the so-called advantages of modern society cannot fill the basic human need for deep, intimate companionship and personal meaning in life. For between the rounds of "liberated" social activities and between the stepping stones to professional achievement skulk the spectres of a lonely present and a lonelier future. These spectres are already constant companions of many a quietly desperate single person.

Our problems as single adults are real and complex. But they are not all necessarily caused by our singleness. After my sister-in-law—happily married—heard me expound on the problems and temptations of the single woman, she said, "Married people also struggle with these same problems, but in different ways." Other married friends have said the same. Loneliness, for example. We wish we had someone to welcome us home, someone who would listen eagerly to all the details of our day and give support and comfort. But even marriage doesn't guarantee that. A husband may be too preoccupied with his own job or a wife too overwhelmed with the problems of the children to listen to the other person. Each needs attention; neither has any to give. Or a husband may have to travel, coming home only for weekends. Then both partners live a lonely life much of the time.

Another problem is the need for sexual intimacy. A single thinks, "If I were married, that delight would be available all the time and there'd be no hassle." But marrieds hasten to clarify this: The physical side, wonderful as it can be, isn't automatically perfect. Individuals have hangups that make a satisfying sexual relationship difficult or (without help) impossible. Then too, one partner may be away or ill. Children get in the way. Other duties demand time. Who says there are no more hassles once you've said "I do"?

The Two Faces of Our Humanness

We have problems basically because we're human. We are imperfect people living in an imperfect world. But let's be sure that we understand both sides of what it means to be human.

One side of humanness includes having problems and needs and the means to act with selfish malice! You and I have often used the after-all-I'm-only-human excuse.

Our pastor, a truly godly friend of many, once told us a

personal incident. He was driving with his family on a highway when another car passing theirs cut in too suddenly and too sharply because of oncoming traffic. Jamming down his brakes, he burst out angrily, "Damn it!" His teen-age daughter gleefully responded, "Oh, Daddy, Daddy, you're human like us!"

This is indeed one side of our humanness; we have indeed been marred by sin. But is that all, even in unredeemed people? No, there is a second side to our humanness, a side that is fine and beautiful.

The other day in this Malaysian mountain town where I'm enjoying a writing holiday, I trekked down to the post office. What a surprise awaited me. The postal clerk, a young Hindu, greeted me: "Good morning. I knew you were coming today, and I brought you roses. I remember how last year you liked them so well." With that he presented me a bountiful bouquet of the magnificent roses for which this area is famed. I gasped at their loveliness and fragrance. But I was even more overwhelmed by his spontaneous thoughtfulness.

When we experience or observe such an act of human kindness, do we say, "Oh, he's human like us"? No, we don't. Yet it is not only pettiness and harshness and twistedness that remain in our humanness. God's Word written in the Bible, on nature and into our experience tells us otherwise. The image of God in man still shows through as well. God is constantly wooing us through thousands of his natural gifts that surround us in order that we might come to him directly and be made wholly human forever.

First-Rate Human Beings

If the gospel of Jesus Christ says (and it does) that no case is hopeless, no state is unredeemable on earth, no problem is too hard for God, then why are there so many frustrated, despairing and life-denying single men and women? We find them not only in society as a whole but even among Christians. I don't think we've worked *together* hard enough in this delicate, misunderstood area.

Often there is restraint, if not silence, on the subject. Or a studied casualness. Sometimes in the "total church program" the place of the single adult is an awkward afterthought. We ask them to teach Sunday school, to be camp counselors or cooks, committee members—and then we're satisfied that we have provided "healthy outlets" for them. Or we expect them to take on lots of responsibility because, after all, "they have lots of extra time and energy." We don't really know what their lives are like.

But many single adults would love to talk about the subject more honestly with married people if they could. They would love to be treated not merely as helpful church members but as the first-rate human beings that they are by God's grace!

In the following chapters let us objectively and compassionately try to see the different sides of reality on this subject. Reality about the unmarried state includes (1) the facts from God's viewpoint—the biblical teaching on singleness, (2) the facts of our human experience—problems and temptations, (3) the facts underlying the possibility of a satisfying, happy and useful life—creativity and maturity and (4) the facts about Jesus Christ—the Man who was God.

BIBLICAL TEACHING ON SINGLENESS

2

Yes, there is clear biblical teaching on singleness. Let's try to look at the facts from God's viewpoint.

Most single women would not say out loud as one friend of mine bluntly did, "God doesn't really care about me, or else he would have given me a husband." But that is what many *feel* deep down within. As we deal with this super-sensitive subject of singleness, biblical teaching alone does not heal the wounds that may be there. We confront overpowering feelings. What can we do?

Do we simply say to ourselves, "Now stop feeling that way," and expect the feeling to be gone with the wind? No, for we cannot command our emotions. But we can suggest directions to our emotions. We do this by what we feed our minds, which eventually influence our emotions.

Think Right

For instance, suppose we keep thinking, "I would have had a better start in life if my parents had been better educated." The emotional result may be resentment against our parents and a deepened sense of personal inadequacy. But suppose we counter that negative (and unfair) thought with this truth: "God gave me my parents, and they've brought me up in the best way they knew. God has also built into me immense potential which he wants to help me develop."

The emotional result will be a positive feeling about ourselves that then moves us to a position of strength to face the problems. We will be able to work creatively with the Lord to become a full human being. And we will also come to appreciate our parents for who they are and what they have done for us in providing a better education for us than they themselves had.

In the same way, if we keep feeding our minds negative or downright wrong ideas about God and ourselves as single women, we will eventually be burdened with the dead weight of sick emotions. We'll resent God. We'll hate ourselves. We'll envy other people's happiness.

We need more objectivity on this subject for we tend to be most subjective in discussing marriage and/or the unmarried state—everyone is an authority! The topic touches the rawest core of our being.

But Scripture and the collaboration of history and personal experience give clear instructions about what God does indeed say concerning his original purpose for man, his intentions for marriage and his redemption of the single state.

God's Original Purpose for Man: Marriage

Anyone looking at our confused world could conclude that if there is a God, either he does not care about the human mess or he is helpless to do anything about it. A frustrated single woman is tempted to apply this same conclusion to her personal situation: God goofed.

From what we can learn in the Bible about life on earth, marriage was the natural state God intended for every man and woman. Genesis 1—2, reflecting God's original purposes for man, does not debate marriage as optional but assumes it as natural. Together man and woman were to use and control the earth environment which God had lovingly prepared for them (Gen. 1:26-31). How much this one charge implies! How wonderful that God conceived a most glorious plan for his creature children, that he endowed them with intellectual powers and personal ability to carry out that plan and that he arranged for them to find fulfillment in doing a good job of it!

But we need only look at life gone wrong because of our human rebelliousness and our own inhumanity to our fellow men—corrupt governments, growing terrorism, delinquent parents, environmental pollution, energy crisis, broken relationships—to know that we simply do not live in an ideal world.

The ideal world would have a husband for every woman. But what do we find instead? Earlier male deaths reduce the prospective population. And wars—the Vietnam war, which stretched over nearly three decades, cut off thousands of young men from young Vietnamese women. What hope have they now for marriage and a family? For other reasons we find the average church also with a heart-breaking ratio of young men to young women. Moreover, the latter often complain that even the remnant has no appeal.

This is the first stark reality we must accept: We live in an imperfect world where the ratio of men to women is imperfect.

God's Intention for Marriage

Now we face the next difficulty: How can a single woman or man attain the human fulfillment that marriage is intended to bring? In fact, *can* an unmarried person be fully human? First, let us take a closer look at the biblical teaching on God's intention for the union of a man and a woman.

According to Genesis 1 and 2, God intended marriage to be the complementary union of a man and a woman for (1) communal living, (2) fulfillment of male and female sexuality, (3) partnership in using and controlling their environment and (4) perpetuation of the human race.

Yet rarely in these days do we witness God's intention for married people being positively carried out. Rather we observe a growing number of hell-on-earth marriages. I was staggered to read a statement by a seminary professor: "I know personally twenty-nine of our alumni whose marriages are on the rocks because of women in their churches."[1] So an imperfect world produces not only unwanted spinsterhood but also unfulfilled and broken marriages. Thus a single woman would be unrealistic in supposing that marriage would automatically bring her the happiness and the joy and fulfillment of all her basic human needs.

Moreover, God's Word does not teach that marriage in itself is the highest goal in life. Jesus said, "You are wrong, because you know neither the scriptures nor the power of God. For in the resurrection they neither marry nor are given in marriage, but are like angels in heaven" (Mt. 22:29-30).

Jesus' statement has several implications (besides the possible warning that a man should not call any woman an angel lest he imply she is a sexless being!). The first is that marriage is not an eternal state, though obviously it leaves lasting imprints on one's personality. It is a beautiful, temporal arrangement for earthly living, a marvelous idea from God.

The second implication is that marriage is a life within a life—a specialized, personal union of two lives on earth within the greater context of eternal living. Likewise, the single Christian woman lives out her singleness within the greater context of eternal living. All of God's people share in this greater, more real life from God.

The third implication is that this greater eternal life, not marriage, is to be our highest fulfillment in all existence. Jesus Christ said, "And this is eternal life, that they know thee the only true God, and Jesus Christ whom thou hast sent" (Jn. 17:3). So it is what I do with my life in relation to the eternal God that counts in the long run. It is how responsibly I live out my earthly life—married or single—within this larger life that determines my ultimate personal worth and fulfillment. What God really cares about is not my marital status but what I am doing with what I have and how I relate to my fellow beings.

Despite the mess the world has become, God is not frustrated in his purposes—for mankind in general, for marriage in the concrete or for the remnant of the singles. Hebrews 2:5-18 explains this. I think this passage is the most magnificent statement of Jesus' humanity in the whole Bible. The writer says that God's "Plan A," man's care and control of the earth, had to be set aside because man had become irresponsible. It has been superseded by "Plan B," Jesus' control of the earth. Man gets a second chance. God is still sovereign.

Redemption is what the Bible and Christianity are all about. Christians can cheerfully accept the imperfections and sufferings of this often desperate existence because they know it is only a temporary state. They believe that Jesus Christ through his death and resurrection became Redeemer-Lord of all, including both marriage and singleness.

This is why discipled Christians, married or single, keep working actively with the Lord to hasten the end of this imperfect existence in society, as well as in the personal lives of men and women. They're moving along in God's stream of history toward the concrete realization of his kingdom.

The Power of Choice

It seems to me there are three directions a single woman can choose for her life.

First, she can live in a perpetual state of tension and frustration. When she mistrusts a good and loving God, her life becomes one long, boring complaint to others. This is self-defeating, for the result makes her most unattractive to men, women and children!

Second, she can resign herself to a sub-woman's existence. She becomes afraid to appear gentle, warm, womanly. She denies her creatureliness, her feminine gender. Thus in essence she denies the good Creator who made her and still wants the best for her. These unwholesome denials of life lead to a grey-brown, shriveled-up leaf of a life or to an artificial life with false compensations.

Or, third, she can accept her present status as the one God fully purposes for her fulfillment as a woman. In fact, she can offer it back to him freely and gladly. This does not mean she does not think about marriage or find (some) men attractive. She can be honest with the Lord about her desires. She can trust his sovereign goodness. He very well may have marriage for her later. But no matter what the final marital result may be, she *cannot* lose as a person.

God's Redemptive Gift of Being Single

The third direction is clearly based on a strong biblical foundation. Apart from Jesus, Paul the apostle, although a man, was a prime example. Some think he was a misogynist, but that is to read the record carelessly.

Paul said,

I wish that all were as I myself am [single]. But each has his own special gift from God, one of one kind and one of another. . . . I want you to be free from anxieties. The unmarried man is anxious about the affairs of the Lord, how to please the Lord. . . . And the unmarried woman or girl is anxious about the affairs of the Lord, how to be holy in body and spirit. (1 Cor. 7:7, 32, 34)

A gift is to be used and enjoyed. What an insult to the giver if we criticize and object to the gift he has given in thoughtfulness and love! One Christmas in our university days my sister gave me a gift. She had worked for two weeks during that holiday to earn the money. I later learned she had spent every dollar and cent she earned to pay for the costly, leatherbound chain reference Bible which she knew I could use both then and in a future ministry.

Never have I been given a more sacrificial gift. And yet I was disappointed. I had been wanting a new coat or at least a cashmere sweater. It was not until several years later that I learned to use that chain reference Bible fruitfully for myself and with others. Then the gift became real and meaningful. And my sister's love became more precious.

Likewise for a long time I did not consider that my single status was a gift from the Lord. I did not resent it—to be frank, in my earlier idealistic period I thought that because I had chosen singleness I was doing God a favor! But in later years I was severely tested again and again on that choice. Then, through Paul's words and life and my subsequent experiences, it gently dawned on me that God had given me a superb gift!

Once this truth took root in me I felt my personality becoming more and more liberated. I found myself stretching out more eagerly and confidently for life. Instead of fatalistically accepting singleness as God's impersonal will, I gladly volunteered it back to him for his wise disposal. And he has not been my debtor; he has lavished his love and wealth on me.

Then I came to understand in depth what Jesus meant when he said,

That [refraining from marriage] is something which not everyone can accept, but only those for whom God has appointed it. For while some are incapable of marriage because they were born so, or were made so by men, there are others who have themselves renounced marriage for the sake of the kingdom of Heaven. Let those accept it who can. (Mt. 19:11-12, NEB)

The most important issue for an unmarried woman is not, "How can I find a husband so that I may be happy?" It is, rather, "How can I live out the creative life that God intended in love for all men and women to have?" This is neither to say that we repress any hope for marriage in God's gracious will nor that we refuse to face the agonizing problems inherent in the unmarried state. Rather it is to affirm that both our natural desire for marriage and all of our problems in not being married are under the control of a compassionate Creator-Lord.

PROBLEMS AND TEMPTATIONS OF A SINGLE WOMAN
3

The problems and temptations we now discuss are not peculiar to a single woman. They are present in all kinds of other human beings. But we singles have to guard against them in a special way. There are many—some obvious, some subtle.

Self-Rejection

The basic problem of many, many single women is that gnawing away at their self-respect is a feeling of shame. They feel men have bypassed them because they are undesirable as women. They question their sexuality. They begin to form a false image of themselves. They reject their own persons.

Perhaps they have forgotten, or never known, this tender

and profound truth straight from God's own heart, not only historically to Israel but also personally to them as individuals:

But now thus says the Lord,
>he who created you, O Jacob,
>he who formed you, O Israel:

"Fear not, for I have redeemed you;
>I have called you by name, you are mine.

When you pass through the waters I will be with you;
>and through the rivers, they shall not overwhelm you;

when you walk through fire you shall not be burned,
>and the flame shall not consume you.

For I am the LORD your God,
>the Holy One of Israel, your Saviour.

I give Egypt as your ransom,
>Ethiopia and Seba in exchange for you.

Because you are precious in my eyes,
>and honoured, and I love you,

I give men in return for you,
>peoples in exchange for your life." (Is. 43:1-4)

You and I are infinitely precious to God. We must not let Satan or the world or circumstances convince us otherwise. And God can become infinitely precious to us.

Guilt Feelings

Sometimes a woman who feels rejected by men also feels guilty. She has a vague feeling that she has done something wrong to deserve such a "fate." This may be pseudo-guilt. (As one fellow said, "It could also be that men have just been too stupid.") But every guilt has to be dealt with, real or pseudo. For her guilt feelings will destroy her relationships and disintegrate her personality. She needs to bring them all to the Lord. Then she will know that Calvary's permanent healing and relief cover not only conscious, personal sin, but also the grief and sorrow sometimes inflicted by others (see Is. 53:4-5). Jesus took on our sins, and our griefs and sorrows as well.

As the psalm says:

Blessed is he whose transgression is forgiven,
  whose sin is covered.
Blessed is the man to whom the Lord imputes no iniquity,
  and in whose spirit there is no deceit. (Ps. 32:1-2)

Brittleness

Once in a while I look at the mirror reflectively. I am sometimes disturbed to see hard lines creeping into my features. Then I have to pray, "Lord, make me gentle and flexible, as I'm not naturally inclined to be, but as I can be by your grace." Our instinct for self-preservation may cause us to defend our ego, our choices, our lifestyle. Private rationalizations about secret habits or extravagant compensations nurture those facial furrows. What has happened? We have tried to make ourselves invulnerable.

It is unavoidable that we single women develop independence and decisiveness, sometimes more than our married sisters who have husbands to decide for or with them. But what is avoidable is the defensive brittleness and strident voice that often accompany female independence.

In any country I move into for a few weeks or months for

student ministry, I am under the national male leadership. Nine out of ten times the men are younger than I. (In one case the general secretary of the student movement was half my age!) Yet I believe that what Peter told wives about being gentle and submissive applies equally to me as a single woman in relationships with men. I don't say it's easy, especially when one must consider how the biblical principle should be applied in various cultures—from extremely permissive societies in the West to extremely conservative cultures where women have just emerged from behind their veils. But I don't know any double biblical standard for the behavior of single women and of married women. The challenge is to be submissive when necessary, take initiative when necessary, lead when necessary and always maintain "the imperishable jewel of a gentle and quiet spirit, which in God's sight is very precious" (1 Pet. 3:4).

Self-Orientation

Every human being begins life self-oriented. But as we mature, our world begins to include others. Family living forces us to consider others' needs and wishes. But when one lives a single life, the tendency to be preoccupied with self is in danger of being reinforced. Weekends are used, furniture is chosen, money is spent, holidays are planned basically with regard only to oneself. One does not have to consider what others want.

It is possible to become so accustomed to making decisions with regard only to one's own desires that one thinks all decisions can be made that way. Then, in a group it can be difficult for a single person to see an issue from someone else's viewpoint or to work cooperatively with others for a greater common goal. Any decision that does not benefit *me* must surely be wrong!

Loneliness

Loneliness can be particularly acute for a single woman because of this tendency toward self-centered living. She may be living with her family or with other single women—but often this very situation aggravates her loneliness. It is the emotional isolation she feels within. She would naturally prefer an intimate relationship with one person, a husband, to whom she could express herself fully as a woman, in tenderness and self-giving.

But she should know that even the intimate companionship of marriage cannot be an end in itself. No partners in such a relationship can find lasting satisfaction unless together they give themselves to higher values and goals outside themselves. In the same way the unmarried woman can overcome loneliness only by giving herself to others around her and to life at her doorstep. She must learn to live by values outside her own self-gratification.

Sex

It is usually easier to compensate or sublimate in other areas than in the physical need for sexual expression and satisfaction. It is in this area that one can become most agonizingly frustrated. And if the frustration is not resolved, it can turn to twistedness or bitterness.

But it is also here that the God who created our sex energies and physical appetites proves himself most understanding and sufficient. If a single woman learns to handle this realistic problem by God's grace and some rugged discipline, it will affect every other part of her personality in beautiful, life-affirming ways. Of this, as of the other problems and temptations, we say more in the following chapter.

Anxiety about Relating to Men

Once while working for a brilliant but absent-minded lawyer I had to remind him three times to sign some important documents. He finally did, saying, "I bet you think I'd make a terrible husband." Since he was happily married and my heart was decidedly elsewhere, I answered, "The thought never occurred to me." He said, "Oh, yes, it has. Every woman consciously or unconsciously measures every man she meets according to her ideal of a husband."

I think he was almost right. The problem for us single women is how to control this tendency so it does not make us self-conscious or calculating in our friendships with the opposite sex!

Eligible Christian bachelors may be tempted to think that all single females, who may outnumber them ten to one in certain communities, are eyeing them more as predatory hawks than as peaceful doves. Sometimes they are not far from being right! But often they are so guarded in their relationships with women that it increases the awkwardness for all.

Worry about the Future

An unmarried woman visiting a noisy, messy home overrun with children and their "junk" may be glad she does not have to live in that pandemonium. She may also be secretly glad she does not have to put up with "that uncooperative husband" about whom her friend sometimes complains. As she considers how noise pollution adversely affects the health and nervous system, she may honestly prefer her quiet and privacy without a family. Moreover, she can also be glad that she doesn't have to bring up teen-agers in an increasingly permissive society where experiments with drugs, the occult and sexual freedom exert such a pull.

But she also has anxious periods of wondering whether she may be even more alone in the future than now. Who will be concerned when she's old? Where will be the companion to share her retirement? What will happen when she gets sick? Where will be the grown children to care for her?

Quiet Plans of Love

We all have friends who live with these problems and temptations in one degree or another. Once I spent hours and days with one. She had a good position with lifetime security. But she was unmarried, soon unyoung and very unhappy. We talked long and intensively about the problem—herself. She was highly intelligent, so that she could intellectually argue against nearly anything I said. We were going in circles. She knew it. I knew it.

Afterward I began to wonder again how to help people like her. I knew it was not just a matter of giving good advice. But as I pondered the ramifications, I temporarily concluded that many things in life are simply imponderable.

The next day I went to Bangkok. As usual I visited the bookstore as soon as I could. This time as I entered, a new item caught and held my eye. Designed with a traditional pattern on deep pink Thai silk, the motto read:

God is
silently planning
for you in love

That was it! That explained adequately the imponderables of life, especially for us singles. It wasn't a verse directly from the Bible. But I remembered vaguely something like it in Jeremiah. Thumbing through my Bible I located it in Jeremiah 29: 11, "For I know the plans I have for you, says the LORD, plans for welfare and not for evil, to give you a future and a hope."

Previously I had written a comment in the margin: "The controls are in God's heart." But now this truth struck with deeper poignancy. Why, I thought, God has his quiet plans of love for us singles no less than for the married people!

People don't usually associate love or being loved with unmarried adults, do they? Maybe it's because some of us make ourselves unlovely and unlovable! But God's plans for a single person are just as important, just as carefully and lovingly thought up as his plans for a married person. And God never makes mistakes in his plans for anyone.

PROSPECTS FOR HAPPINESS AND USEFULNESS

4

What does God want for his children? I received an answer from my mother even before she came to know God personally (at seventy-two!). We nine children have always found it difficult to find appropriate gifts for her. She lives very simply, mainly for the constantly expanding family. So we usually end up getting something *we've* been wanting for the house! Once before Mother's Day we decided to ask her directly what her heart's desire was.

Her reply: "The one thing a mother wants is that her children be happy and useful." I heard those words as though from God himself about his own children.

The single woman who knows she belongs to Jesus Christ has many, many more possibilities than her non-Christian sister has, not only to overcome her problems and temptations, but also to turn these liabilities into happy, useful assets. For she has constant and direct access to "Divine Resources, Unlimited."

If she has not yet learned to draw from God's infinite riches, she can begin now.

Giving Oneself to Christ

First of all, she can find a genuinely intimate relationship with Christ as Savior, Friend and Lord. An acquaintance of mine (male, single) once spoke derisively of Roman Catholic nuns who "treat Jesus as a husband substitute." What he apparently did not understand was that our spirituality is so linked with our sexuality that it is often difficult to separate one from the other.

Flying from Rome to Munich I had warm fellowship with an attractive and spirited nun. I learned this was her first visit home to Germany after thirty years as a missionary. No wonder she was excited! I could also tell that she loved Christ and had served him happily even through the war in the Philippines, where she had been imprisoned in an enemy camp. We talked about our faith in Jesus Christ and our walk with him. Then she showed me her plain gold ring on the inside of which was inscribed, "Wed to Christ." But there certainly was nothing neurotic about her. She was refreshingly human!

Like her, we need feel no restraint in loving Jesus Christ. This love should not only have intelligent respect and determined will, but it should also have hearty affection. This is absolutely fundamental to all of life. I will devote a chapter to it.

Extending Oneself to Others

The Lord knows very well that we also need visible human companionship. "It is not good that the man [or woman] should be alone" (Gen. 2:18). Companionship means not only spouses but all friends whom we need and who need us. No one human person alone can meet all our needs. Not our one best friend, nor even the "perfect husband" or "ideal wife." This is why God provides all kinds of people to help fulfill the many complex needs we human beings have.

One friend may be able to satisfy us intellectually but he may be emotionally cool. Another friend is fun to be with, and we need her light touch but not all the time. Still another well understands us by her ability to project into our heart situation, but she cannot rebuke when we need to be checked.

Friendships will not come by our sitting at home nursing our self-pity. We must go where people are and gently extend ourselves to them. For some of us who are shy, this demands uphill effort at first. But it's necessary, for thus we begin to find our humanness. Much talk has been overflowing these days about understanding yourself, accepting yourself, loving yourself. But we cannot know who we are in a social vacuum. We can only identify our distinct individuality when we relate meaningfully to other individuals.

And we must not neglect the members of our own family. No matter how "awful" they are, they are the only ones we have! Any other kind of happiness is marred if we do not have healthy relationships with them. Even though we may have been terribly hurt by them and would rather avoid or forget them, we cannot. Too much has gone into our lives together already for us to ignore them. Especially with our parents— God wants to help us bridge the gaps of time, culture and lifestyle. Some of us need to learn how to give ourselves back to our families.

Enjoying Children

Children are fascinating little human beings! One of the revered teachers in Martin Luther's childhood town never so much as looked at the adults as he walked down a street. But he always doffed his hat respectfully to every child he met. His explanation was, "I know what adults are like. But who knows what a child will be?"

If one has nieces and nephews, how fortunate! (We have fifteen or sixteen "niblings" in our family.) I have seen many a strained family relationship eased by an unmarried aunt spending time and energy with the children. I think especially of one who unobtrusively planned her weekends and her income so that she could spend time with each successive family among her married brothers and sisters. She was quietly convinced it was her ministry from the Lord. And now after some twenty-five years of this, the family has some of the most heart-warming gatherings I have ever seen. More-over, one by one her agnostic family is coming to Jesus Christ. She has no more leisure hours than other professional women, but she has the motivation, and she plans the time to pray for and to visit them.

It is a great relief to parents for some other person periodically to look after their lively children. This is a solid way of maintaining natural relationships not only with married sisters and brothers, but also with married friends. It's good for the children, and both children and parents appreciate each other more when they are with each other again.

But when we're not sincere, these perceptive little people know it. I was recently in the home of some friends when the five-year-old son returned from kindergarten. His mother asked how he liked his new teacher. He answered, "She smiles all the time, but she doesn't like us."

What kind of aunty or adult friend do children like best to stay overnight with? She's the one who has developed a reputation with them for being fun. She has learned to read and tell stories with their sense of imagination and wonder. She sings fun songs with them. She plans special activities that they enjoy and can anticipate with excitement.

Being a "Nurturant Mother"

I would love to meet a certain Sunday school teacher in Oakland. I was having dinner with a couple when six-year-old Bennett dashed in after his first time in Sunday school. He eagerly asked his parents, "What's Jesus' phone number? I want to talk with him." It was obvious that his new excitement came from a Sunday school teacher who was deeply understanding of children and could make Jesus real and exciting to them. She was complementing the parents' spiritual upbringing of Bennett.

Some of the best mothers I've seen are not the biological

ones but the nurturant ones. They are the childless women who give themselves especially to young people who look to them for help. Teen-agers who are trying to assert their individuality by breaking away from their parents' authority still need guiding authority and counsel. This is why we often see extremely popular youth ministers, young people's advisers and student workers. They stand in that gap.

Singles may be psychologically closer to these young people than their own parents are. Sometimes we may be closer to them spiritually, too, if the parents are not Christians or at least not committed ones. Thus we have an unrepeatable opportunity to help nurture these young folk. God can use us as turning points in their lives.

The New Testament apostles often spoke affectionately of God's local flock as also being their own children. That is how Paul felt about Timothy and Titus. He was their "nurturant father." A nurturant parent's responsibilities are serious. He is responsible to God for these children in the faith.

I do not write this to make you ashamed, but to admonish you as my beloved children. For though you have countless guides in Christ, you do not have many fathers. For I became your father in Christ Jesus through the gospel. I urge you, then, be imitators of me. Therefore I sent to you Timothy, my beloved and faithful child in the Lord, to remind you of my ways in Christ, as I teach them everywhere in every church. (1 Cor. 4:14-17)

Welcoming Everyone and Every New Experience

I still am amazed at times to meet bored people. Life is throbbing in all of nature and in people—and they're bored! There are so many fascinating things to learn and people to know in richer depths in this variegated world God has put us in that we can never in one lifetime learn all. But we can begin and continue into eternity. I'm truly glad we have at least a couple of billion years for this! There's infinite room for personal growth in heaven.

The first commandments God gave to the first man and woman are staggering in their implications of a delegated rulership. "Be fruitful and multiply, and fill the earth and subdue it; and have dominion over . . . every living thing that moves upon the earth" (Gen. 1:28). I think this is how the psalmist also felt when he said,

When I look at thy heavens, the work of thy fingers,
    the moon and the stars which thou hast established;
what is man that thou art mindful of him,
    and the son of man that thou dost care for him?
Yet thou hast made him little less than God,
    and dost crown him with glory and honor.
Thou hast given him dominion over the works of thy
        hands;
    thou hast put all things under his feet,
all sheep and oxen,
    and also the beasts of the field,
the birds of the air, and the fish of the sea,
    whatever passes along the paths of the sea.

O LORD, our Lord,
    how majestic is thy name in all the earth! (Ps. 8:3-9)

But that's not the end of the story. Think of Jesus' conclusion to his famous parable of the talents in Matthew 25:14-30: "Well done, good and faithful servant; you have been faithful over a little, I will set you over much; enter into the joy of your master." Apparently we cannot experience the joy of human fulfillment unless we exercise a certain care and control over the environment God has gifted us with.

This is why we need to develop new interests and hobbies. We need continually to be interested in people, all different kinds of people. We need to know about events going on around us and to be exposing ourselves to new ideas. This is God's wide and wonderful world. We should know it before we leave it for other worlds. Otherwise, heaven may shock us.

We mustn't just stick to our career. Some day that must end. Then what will we have? Now is the time to develop a wholesome attitude to life, and that means being open to all of life pulsating around us.

In country after country some of the most attractive people I meet are single missionaries. They are absolutely the most life-affirming people anywhere. They obviously channel their creative drive and energies to help others around them in Jesus' name. I watch them and I'm inspired! They pour out their emotional energies constructively to encourage people who desperately need understanding and acceptance.

At the same time these same busy people make time for cultural interests with their friends—folk music, brush painting, modern literature, flower arrangements. They don't wait for life to come to them. They go out to meet it with a hearty welcome. No wonder they're such fascinating and likeable people.

Once last year during a month-long student leadership camp we were relaxing. A highlight of the fun night was an Indonesian folk dance by a missionary. What fascinated me was not only that she was from Britain, but also that she had a slight physical deformity which could have made her self-conscious.

She danced with grace and skill that won spontaneous applause and encores. She tossed off our compliments with, "Oh, I just learned this in my spare time with some of my Indonesian friends." I have no doubt that this natural acceptance of herself and willingness to have fun is one of the reasons she and her preaching ministry are so well received in her community.

Thank God You're Normal!

When you begin to feel overpowered by your natural sex desires, stop and thank God that you are human and normal. Thank him that you're full of creative force, for the sex drive is part of every human person's built-in reservoir of basic energies—to be meaningfully related to others, to find purpose in daily work, to develop one's aesthetic capacities, to be rewarded with a sense of achievement. God's people by his grace never need to face a personal energy crisis.

Don't isolate your sexual powers from the rest of your powers by constant mental focus on sex. It is not wrong to read or watch romances; but it is dangerous to keep feeding one's mind with salacious details through any medium (and especially through daydreaming while still in bed). Like masturbation it can lead to greater fantasy and loneliness, among other things.

It helps very, very much to pray realistically on the basis of 1 Corinthians 10:13, "Lord, you made me, so you understand what I'm going through. Help me to accept and understand what my sex and sexuality really mean. You have said that even this sometimes worrisome problem is not beyond what any person can bear. So I take you seriously when you say I can count on you to sustain me as I go through this struggle."

A good way to help relieve the biological sex tensions is to get involved in physical recreation regularly and vigorously. *In fact, this is an absolute necessity.* But even apart from the relief and necessary distraction that exercise gives, we need it for general health. Swim, hike, bowl, play badminton—anything that provides a physical outlet.

Not all of us are inclined toward sports. I'm not. Sometimes the very thought of exercise makes me feel tired even before I begin. But always afterward I feel better. I like myself more. The healthier blood circulation and tightening up of muscles take away sluggishness. I'm more mentally alert. And I understand better what Paul meant when he said that we are to glorify God through our bodies, which are the temples of the Holy Spirit (1 Cor. 6:19-20).

My particular work, being an itinerant one from city to city and country to country, doesn't allow me to be in a regular physical health program. But even in my irregular schedule I know I must make time for either simple Danish calisthenics learned in college or jogging in place (if the floor is concrete and I don't disturb the household).

In most cities and towns one can find physical health programs, especially at the local YWCA. If there aren't any, get together with a few others and organize your own. In Hong Kong some single young adults have had a Mountain and Water Fellowship for several years, which has been wholesome not only for fun and physical exercise but also for evangelism.

Finally, it has been a tremendous help for me to know that Jesus, because he was fully man as well as fully God, basically faced these same problems. When I've been tempted to feel sorry for myself in this area, the greatest help has been to ask, "How did those bachelors, Jesus, Paul, Luke and Barnabas, lick this problem?" The answer in their examples is extremely instructive and inspiring! They vigorously channeled their passions into God's service, in loving and helping people into his kingdom. In America, where we've been brought up on a steady diet of self-gratification, this is difficult but still possible.

Carrying on as a Woman, Not a Female Zombie

Sexual tensions will not always be a problem. The physiological fact is that the drive diminishes (does not disappear) as one reaches the middle years and beyond. But the way one learns to handle this physical/psychological problem as a younger woman will largely determine her emotional health in later years. And should God bring a husband to her, she will have a better marriage if she enters it with a healthy view of herself and of sex.

At any age the single woman needs to respect herself as a sexual being whom God created. She is not less sexual for not being married. *Sex* has to do with the biological drive for union with one of the opposite sex. *Sexuality* has to do with our whole personhood as a woman or a man. It has to do with the way we express ourselves in relation to others. It has to do with being warm, understanding, receptive, sexual beings when we relate to another female or to a child or to a man who is the least prospect for a husband!

In our student ministry I often work with some of the most eligible bachelors in the Christian community (that is, eligible for the younger ladies). Several years ago in a Southeast Asian country such a colleague was being increasingly besieged with volunteer female assistance, office curtains and flowers, as well as parental invitations for negotiations. In concern I advised him, "There are so many lovely Christian girls. Make up your mind and get it over with." In exasperation he replied, "They're all quite feminine, but not one of them is womanly. They're all concerned with appearing pretty, not in being a real woman." (He recently married a real woman who is also lovely.)

Relating to Men Positively

I am sure other women have suggestions on how to maintain healthy relationships with men. I can share only what has been helpful to me. First, I try to look upon every man—young or old, eligible or ineligible—as my fellow human being. He belongs to God, even the non-Christian who does not know that yet. So he is sacred property, not mine to maneuver and manipulate according to *my* wishes or desires.

Second, I try to treat him as I do my two brothers. I enjoy Leon and Dick. I respect them. I like to hear them talk about masculine things in masculine ways. I am pleased when they treat me thoughtfully. But I am not disappointed or resentful when they forget. I realize I do not always act like a lady! I try to be a relaxing friend to them, accepting them as they are.

Now admittedly all of this is relatively easy if the man is your brother or if he simply doesn't appeal to you as someone you'd like to live with the rest of your life. The problem arises when the man is extraordinarily attractive. How can any woman relax in *that* situation? It may be next to impossible, but we must still try to maintain the same relaxed and non-demanding attitude. Otherwise we'll appear either like a female zombie or a female hawk. We should pray that God will control our emotions and our relationships, so that the results are wholesome for all in the long run.

With care and discretion a single woman can and should be a real woman to the men around her. She can with God's wisdom and protection follow the biblical principle of being a "help meet" for them. She has vast reservoirs of love, kindness and understanding dammed up in her. Her role may be as a sister or a mother or a helper or a friend without the tension of romance. This may not be all that she wants, but to be such a friend is far healthier than to be a self-pitying loner. And it certainly is more likely to lead to romance and marriage!

FRIENDSHIPS WITH MARRIED PEOPLE

5

Bachelors can also get discouraged and depressed, I've heard. Even famous ones, like the Apostle Paul. His good friend Luke recorded at least one instance, in Acts 18:1-11. It happened in Corinth.

A Biblical Example
Paul already had had a trying time before coming to Corinth. He arrived from Athens, where he had been philosophically laughed out of town (Acts 17:32). And previous to that possibly traumatic experience, he had been successively thrown out of Philippi, Thessalonica and Berea! And now, seeking initially to plant the gospel in this notoriously immoral seaport town, he met with the same violent opposition from

his own countrymen that he had received from Gentiles.

Though there were some converts, it seems that Paul was deeply discouraged, and perhaps even fearful for his life. For when the Lord spoke to him in a vision, his first words were, "Do not be afraid, but speak and do not be silent; for I am with you, and no man shall attack you to harm you" (Acts 18:9-10).

But not only was the Lord his very real companion. It is instructive to observe that in this personally distressing situation the Lord had prepared human companionship for Paul in a married couple, Priscilla and Aquila. They proved to be friends that Paul could depend on and even live and work with—people who were spiritually discerning and concerned for others (Acts 18:3, 18, 24-28).

Paul, the boldest and most courageous Christian pioneer in history, depended on human companionship. He needed people, just as much as they needed him, for friendship as well as cooperative work. Barnabas, the big-hearted big brother, and probably also Luke, the beloved physician, helped to check and mold Paul as he matured in the ministry. But even the younger men were humanly indispensable to him—Timothy, Titus, John Mark and others.

Intelligent Conversations and Initiative

A single adult needs to develop friendships with different kinds of people, married as well as single. We said in the first chapter that singles long to talk with married people intelligently, personally. We don't mean we wish to be moaning and groaning all the time. We mean we'd like to be ourselves, to discuss any subject from our context without having to feel self-conscious or defensive.

I've been asking various single friends what exactly is the kind of relationship they would like to have with married people. Here are some representative responses, beginning with the negative ones!

"Well, for one thing, I don't like to hear them worrying about their children all the time."

"They shouldn't pity us or make us feel left out of things."

"I wish they wouldn't assume we know nothing about sex!"

"I don't want them to think about us mainly as singles but as individuals."

"Why do they assume we're all frustrated and unfulfilled?"

"I wish they wouldn't make me feel like vomiting when they get all mushy with each other like nobody was around."

"I'd like to feel included naturally in their conversations about their family and children—not just small talk."

"How about Bible study groups in homes where marrieds and singles meet *regularly*. At our church they're always segregating us because they say their problems are different. So we have to shut up."

"Socially I get tired of being with singles all the time. I'd like to go out once in a while with a congenial couple or with a family on camping trips."

"I'd like to sort of belong to a young family. Everybody's old in my family."

How can we constructively build on these suggestions— even the negative ones? Well, for one thing, I wouldn't start organizing a committee for organizing activities! We've all seen enough of these that exhausted themselves before they got off the ground. I'd simply think prayerfully about who I already feel somewhat congenial with and make a positive suggestion to do something together, something that's different and fun. Then carry on from there to something more culturally stimulating.

In other words, whether you're single or married, *you* take the initiative. *You* plan a fun picnic. *You* suggest the ballet coming to town. *You* open your home for a Bible study fellowship. *You* bake a no-occasion special treat and drop it at someone's home.

That Maiden Aunt
It's important to keep sustained relationships, not just invite others for holidays because they have nowhere else to go. One mutually productive way we mentioned in the previous chapter is to adopt an aunt or be an adopted aunt.

The maiden aunt often makes an interesting character in a story, either as a foil for other characters or as the heroine herself. The family may consider her odd but dependable. Or they may think she's a social albatross around their neck. But in these days she can even be regarded as a social asset! Stereotypes aside, this kind of family tie among people who are not blood relations can be a beautiful thing.

A busy society woman, whose husband has a senior executive position in his company, told me this: "We have guests all the time. But the children have no relatives living in our town. So Harold and I deliberately 'adopted' a single woman as their aunt. She's actually someone I've known since university days. She has her own home but comes and goes to our home as she wants to for dinner and other occasions. The children have come to treat her seriously as an aunt, and she treats them responsibly as her nieces and nephews with the give and take that's involved. It's not a superficial relationship and it's mutually beneficial. We thank God for it."

I know several new Christian families (that is, the parents became Christians only recently) who have done the same thing. In their cases they have non-Christian relatives who visit often, and unfortunately the spiritual influence is sometimes bad for the children. I think these young Christian parents are wise to adopt the Christian aunts that they have —not only for the children, but as one father said, "for us parents, too!"

I observed this same kind of relationship from the aunt's side. On a trip to the States I was to stay for a week with a certain family. How surprised I was upon arrival at their home to be greeted by the children but not the parents. They were away on their vacation! My (single) friend, who had actually made the hospitality arrangements for me, was the "resident aunt" during that vacation time—the first vacation for the parents without the children.

It was fascinating to watch her calmly running the household and going off to work each day as usual. In between she was completely with the young teen-agers, talking with them, discussing their homework, disciplining them, but always enjoying them like thinking adults. Being selfless like that wasn't sacrificial for her. It was a natural part of her glad discipleship under Jesus Christ.

Marriage Agents?

Sometimes married friends trying to be thoughtful are scripturally thoughtless when they say, "Never mind, there's still hope. Mary just got married, and *she's* almost forty!" There seems to be the assumption that the single state is inferior to the married state and that the single woman remains unfulfilled until she marries, as though she were in an existential limbo. A Christian should know better than to believe *that* about God.

But what about married couples "helping out" by introducing prospectives to each other or providing opportunities to get better acquainted with each other in their homes? I think it's an excellent idea, providing it is not an obvious strain on anyone. Simply make sure there are plenty of good conversation and interesting activities so no one will be self-conscious.

Only last week in Singapore I met for the first time the happy husband of an old New Zealand friend I hadn't seen for years. They had met each other at a dinner in the home of mutual friends. He said, "I watched her play with the children. And a strange new thought came to my mind— why, she'd make a good mother." Now twelve years later they have three children of their own.

The Professional Woman and Male Colleagues

One of my married sisters some time ago said to me, "When

you professional women get married, you'll probably marry a widower, because any unmarried man of your age probably has some real sex hang-ups." It seems my time has come and gone! But a number of my contemporaries and colleagues have indeed married widowers with teen-age or grown children. They're happily settled now, and we warmly rejoice with them. Obviously, though, this is not necessarily the answer for everyone.

Often a woman finding genuine fulfillment in life not only in her chosen career but in healthy friendships and cultural pursuits may face another kind of possible tension. It comes in sustained and warm relationships with her married male colleagues.

The female colleague may not have any romantic appeal for the man. But he may sincerely appreciate her professional help and thoroughly enjoy her intellectual stimulation. So when he mentions her at home often and with enthusiasm, his wife (especially if she is already feeling personally inadequate) can begin to be jealous.

This very kind of situation may indicate that the wife is so tied down with housework and children that she has little opportunity for intellectual and cultural activities or that her busy husband is taking her for granted. But there are constructive ways to solve these sorts of problems. We can be truly and directly helpful to both the man and his wife if we spend time with her. We can relieve her suspicions and perhaps our interest in her can even boost her sagging feelings of self-worth. It's always worth every effort to develop friendships with the wives of our colleagues.

On Being Sensitive

A sensitive married couple can have unique opportunities to build up self-respect and feelings of worthiness in single women. They can encourage them in their gifts and potential, their uniqueness, their contributions to community life, their womanly qualities. But they mustn't overdo it—we're sensitive to that! And they shouldn't let the hard independence of some single women throw them off. Some have this exterior because they really are terribly vulnerable within. Yes, they're self-sufficient, but they still need love and warmth.

I often think gratefully of Bill and Libby. Bill was the pastor of our church. They were a handsome couple with six gorgeous children. Their open house simply burst with love for each other and others. Everyone felt it was a treat to go there—Christians and non-Christians, rich and poor, ex-convicts and university professors. It was a clean, well-ordered, lovely home, yet full of spontaneous fun and activities. By both their practical, humble counsel and their obvious example they have directly inspired more Christian marriages and homes than any other couple I have known.

And yet it was this same couple whom God used to help so many of us unmarried women in the community—to help us not only to re-evaluate our single status in an enlightening way but also to enjoy being women. He would sometimes casually comment on something new or flattering we were wearing or express sincere enthusiasm for our unique contributions. Libby, happy and nearly ideal as wife and mother, would sometimes articulate her sincere envy of our greater freedom to do certain things for the Lord and his kingdom or other advantages of being single.

They were real people. Genuine. They naturally but discreetly shared with us their realistic problems of marriage and bringing up children. It wasn't done in a phony way ("We'll share our secrets so you'll see how honest we are"), but in an authentic way that drew us together in true fellowship. When they talked appreciatively about the wonder of being a woman, we singles felt definitely included!

GROWING OLDER WITH WISDOM
6

What will I be like at forty-five?" I began to ask this question, I think, when I was about twelve. At that time I saw a family friend turn from a friendly, smiling woman into a "bitch of a witch," as some said. I heard them say it was because she was going through the change of life that comes to all women around their mid-forties. Some even said she might have to be "put away" at the mental hospital on the other side of the island. It was all a bit vague to me. But that was my introduction to menopause, some of its facts and some of its myths.

But I also observed that not all women her age became depressed, bitchy and witchy. I began to be conscious of how differently people grow older. Perhaps also I unconsciously began to prepare for that inevitable time in my own life!

Age is so relative, isn't it? When I was fifteen I thought middle age was between thirty and thirty-five. Now thirty is so young! And I used to think that one was pretty useless after fifty. Now I am fascinated by people like Ellsworth Bunker, who resumed his diplomatic career at seventy-three, taking on the tough ambassadorial assignment in Saigon. And David Bruce, the first American diplomatic consul to Peking since Chairman Mao Tse-tung and his party took over. Bruce was then seventy-five. And Martha Graham, a world famous figure in modern dance. At eighty she choreographed and supervised what she called the most ambitious season she had ever undertaken. She herself last danced on the stage in 1969, when she was seventy-five. Then a few months ago I read in the newspaper of a little sixty-seven-year-old grandmother who jogged from Tokyo to her birthplace in southwestern Japan—one thousand miles away! It took her five years, sometimes jogging twenty miles a day. But said she, "I trained six years for this."

Transitional Wrecks After Forty

I once asked a good friend in her mid-thirties if she ever gave thought to growing older.

"Yes," she replied. "But I don't like to."

"Why?"

"Oh-h-h," she hesitated. Then with a courageous lift, "It's already lonely, and it's going to get lonelier."

From all outward appearances, one wouldn't think that of her. At any social gathering, whether she's the hostess or the guest, she's alive to people. She has every material thing her heart desires, complete financial security—but apparently no personal security.

I'm concerned about young women like her. They're Christians, and yet an eager responsiveness to life does not characterize them. I want to shout out, "God doesn't want you to stay that way! Everything about life with him is completely opposite from living out your years in growing dread. Life with him is vital interest and continuing curiosity about our environment—our physical environment, our cultural environment, our people environment."

Paul Tournier, in his book *Learn to Grow Old,* which I heartily recommend to *everyone* at any age, studied this subject for several years. He quotes two sociologists who have researched in this area. Dumazedier and Ripert say that if a person is not socially integrated by thirty to forty years of age, it will be impossible between fifty and sixty.[2]

Why is mid-life a crisis for many? Why is it not a crisis for others? I think it's because the former have not really understood life as a whole while the latter do. Carl Jung speaks of the two parts of a person's life. During the first half, by the very nature of his physical youthfulness, a person is strongly biologically oriented. So he "expands" his life and seeks to make something of it. During the second half, when his physical powers are diminishing, a person should be more culturally oriented. He should be developing and enjoying deeper life interests.

The tragedy is that many are not able to make this transitional move from the biological sphere to the cultural sphere.

Their ships founder and wreck.

Recently a doctor related to me a sad story that illustrates quite different emphasis. He described an older woman who had been so exclusively "spiritually" oriented in early life that she was unable to make the transition to old age. She and her husband had been greatly used by God in earlier years. They had helped to establish churches that are still thriving today. She had thrown herself into the work of the church. But she developed no cultural interests. After her husband died and younger leaders were active in the churches, she herself seemed to die within. She is still a sincere believer, loving the Lord and reading her Bible every day. But she knows nothing else to do. She has begged this Christian doctor to give her some kind of drug so she can die quickly and quietly.

Western education lays great emphasis on preparing the child to be an adult. (Indeed, this has come to such an extreme in America that from earliest training a child learns to be fiercely competitive.) One of Tournier's basic questions in his book is: Why don't we have training courses to prepare adults to become older persons? Who's to do it, I don't know. Obviously it's needed. But meanwhile we personally can do much to check the health of our own attitudes to growing older.

Resistance to Growing Older

The con men on Madison Avenue have surely duped our modern society and shaped our values. They have thoroughly convinced many that the chief end of life is to stay young physically. And they have to convince us because million-dollar industries pay them tens of thousands to do so.

Whenever I see a photo or read of a famous (infamous to some) international woman who looks almost ageless in her seventh decade, I feel sad for her. It seems to be well-known that she periodically undergoes cosmetic surgery as one of her many efforts to look young. Perhaps if some of us had her millions and leisure, we might do the same!

Yet are we not virtually doing the same when we try in devious ways to hide our age? Are we ashamed of all the years God has given us?

Now there's nothing wrong with youthfulness. In fact, there's much that is good, right and desirable about it. (See Eccles. 11:9; Jer. 2:2; 1 Tim. 4:12.) How often and with what appeal God speaks of the attractive devotion of Israel or a believer when he was young! King David spoke positively of youth when he praised the steadfast love of God, "who satisfies you with good as long as you live so that your youth is renewed like the eagle's" (Ps. 103:5).

And this is precisely it. David was not talking about physical youthfulness. He was using "youth" as a metaphor for vital energy, alertness, openness to life. The Hebrew word for a young person, *naar,* literally means "growing." Is this not what we mean when we speak admiringly of an older person as being youthful? He's still growing.

Likewise when we use the term "aged," we are speaking metaphorically. We are describing someone who is characterized by inactivity, listlessness, disinterest in life. So there are youthful oldsters and senile adolescents.

We sin against ourselves when we resist growing older. For this resistance is completely unrealistic, since growing older is an inevitable process that no one can reverse. I know no one growing younger. But growing older is not an unhappy "fate" to be endured stoically until one dies bravely. A Christian has every inspiration to keep living fully to the end of his earthly life, for his eternal life continues without a break. The sixty, seventy, eighty years on earth that God may give to us are just the prelude to the next five billion years—and more than that. But it's a terribly important prelude, for our basic character gets set now for heaven, the other side of eternity, where we keep growing.

When we try to hide our age by dyeing our grey hair, wearing teen styles unbecoming to our age and in general behaving like immature young people, in effect we are contradicting God himself. For God says old age is beautiful: "The glory of young men is their strength, but the beauty of old men is their grey hair" (Prov. 20:29).

God doesn't say that old age is better than youth or vice versa. He has so ordained our existence that we go through seasons of life. Each season has its attractions and its distractions. (Reflect on Eccles. 3:1-15, especially the latter half.) At any point we should know the season of our life and live thoughtfully according to that season, just as we do the chronological seasons of winter, spring, summer and autumn.

One day as I was having my hair cut at the beauty salon, a noisy and colorful matron breezed in and sat next to me. "A new style, madame?" the manageress asked her. "Yes, just give me the latest thing coming out of Paris." Whether it looked good or not, she was determined to be youthful and chic!

When we concentrate our powers on delaying or hiding the physical appearances of growing older, we are misdirecting energies that ought to be poured into activities that are truly lasting and truly beautiful. These are not the physical and the transient, but the cultural and the spiritual. They are not self-absorbed but people-related interests. Let's not cheat ourselves of the best things that God has for us.

Advantages of the Mid-Life Period

I sincerely look forward to my fiftieth birthday, if God allows. There's something joyously celebrative about the fiftieth year in anything, even when it's not a golden wedding anniversary. So far in life together with the Lord, the adventure quotient has been so high and exciting that I can't visualize ever disengaging from life or disrelating from people.

Lately I've been asking the alert middle-age friends I meet (notice I now call the fifties *middle* age!) what advantages they are finding in this period of life.

"People don't scare me anymore, so I enjoy them more."

"I've stopped experimenting with life and am now living it and loving it."

"I understand and accept myself more than I did as a younger person."

"I know better what I like to do and forget the other things."

"I've learned to accept the realities of life and can live more comfortably with them."

"I'm not frustrated about my limitations and failures as I used to be, and can now concentrate on my strengths."

"I can witness more confidently to the grace of God."

"I have more time to be quiet and reflect on how best to spend the rest of my life."

"I'm more informed about life. I'm wiser from my mistakes."

"There's more to God than I thought. Christ has become more interesting."

"I can look back and see that the fads in philosophy and theology have come and gone, leaving the Bible intact."

"I'm more relaxed because I've stopped competing with other women and don't try frantically to keep up with fashions and promotions."

"I'm more confident about real values and living by them."

"I get more excited about what else life has in store for me."

I wrote to a friend for her viewpoints which I value because of her life of complete self-giving to others for the sake of God's kingdom. She has been refined by suffering. At the same time she has maintained steady growth in full-orbed creativity as a person. She'll never be famous by man's standards, but she's fruitful in God's books. Here's her answer: "In middle age I have a kind of freedom I have not known earlier—freedom from trying to please others. I can be more truly myself without being bound by people's expectations. E. [another middle-age woman] and I both think we now enjoy a life enriched by experiences that make us wiser in making choices. We know better what are of primary importance, what are secondary and what are only peripheral.

"Did you know that Carl Jung's works were directed towards middle-age people? He says at this age we are more religious. This is because we have become disenchanted with our wordly pursuits. Try to read more of him.

"I think in middle age we know better who we are; we're not like uneasy teens who try to be somebody but usually end up being like everybody—as seen in their quickness to conform.

"One bit of good advice I heard from Anne Baxter [a movie actress]: 'Savor every good moment you have at the time you're having it.' We spend so much time regretting the past, or wishing for better things in the future, that we fail to enjoy the blessings of the present. If you're watching a sunset, enjoy it fully, instead of guiltily saying to yourself, 'Oh, I shouldn't be doing this. I should be home doing the laundry.' If you're spending time with a friend, be with her completely and enjoy the time together.

"It's another way of saying what Jim Elliot did: 'Live to the hilt every situation you know is God's will.'[3] You once told me, 'If we can't trust God radically now, when will we ever?' I think it's the same principle here. If we can't enjoy a conversation, a sunset, reading, listening to music now, when will we ever?

"Perhaps what I'm saying is that the advantage of middle age is that knowing we have fewer years left of life, we tend to make the most of each day."

Before Forty

Of course, these middle-age friends did not suddenly adopt

these attitudes when someone told them "Life begins at forty." Their positive outlooks are the fruit of years of mental, social and emotional discipline.

Other middle age people have very negative attitudes to their present and future life. They are bored with life or increasingly fearful of it. They're pessimistic about themselves and other people. They have few friends and narrow or shallow interests. These also are the fruit of years of certain life habits and responses.

Unless a woman at twenty-five consciously works at changes in her patterns of living, she will have basically the same mental habits, emotional reflexes and life interests at forty. "As now, so then" ought to be placarded on the walls of her mind and especially reconsidered with each succeeding birthday.

If you are a young adult reading this and have not yet seriously thought about the kind of person you want to be at forty, start *now* and work toward it. Caring about what's going on in God's world, continuing to read broadly and reflect on what one has read and observed, retaining a child's sense of wonder and curiosity, maintaining an adventuresome spirit for trying new experiences and keeping interested in people and our common humanity—these are ways of growing till the end of life on this side of eternity. Binding all is Jesus Christ, our human model as well as our sovereign Creator. His example for us as growing people is critical. The next chapter will give it fuller treatment.

Several of my friends who have never been "the athletic type" have just begun to learn to ski. Oh, they'll never make the Olympics. They're in their late thirties. But they've become more alert people for it's been good for them not only physically but psychologically. In our family several of us started to draw and paint only after thirty-five—and my mother began at seventy-four. Work out that secret desire!

"Nothing try, nothing gain." Aristotle Onassis once said that this had been his life motto as he progressed from being a poorly educated laborer to becoming one of the richest men in the world. I certainly am not commending his lifestyle or values. But I do get provoked with some Christians who talk about having the very life of the Creator-God in them and yet who do not express even one-tenth of the vitality and interest in life around them that a person of the world like Onassis did.

Eleanor Roosevelt had an incredibly complex-nurturing adolescence and a marriage that made her suffer inferiority even more as a wife and mother. Yet she eventually became one of the great, creative women of our century. In her late sixties, she was asked the secret of her seemingly limitless strength for accomplishing so much, especially in helping people. Her reply was, "I never waste time and energy in hesitation or regret."

Even better is the way that Paul the apostle put it, because he was absolutely clear about the goal that urged him forward: "Forgetting what lies behind and straining forward to what lies ahead, I press on toward the goal for the prize of the upward call of God in Christ Jesus" (Phil. 3:13-14).

When Jesus Christ is not only her source, but clearly her goal in life, no woman dreads old age.

Menopause and All That Mess

My sister and I once asked our mother what it was like when she went through her menopause. She was genuinely puzzled about our question. Having been brought up in a different culture in China, she hadn't heard that women were supposed to go through the (apparently Western) female trauma of "change of life." She hadn't heard that she should have feared losing her sexuality and gaining a mustache or that she should have hot flashes, unreasonable crying spells, insomnia, growing depression and all those other symptoms. She knew nothing about her ovaries no longer producing as much of the female hormone estrogen as they had during her child-bearing period. She told us, "It just stopped. That's all." She kept on with life and living.

How much unnecessary anxiety menopause myths have caused to many an emotionally fragile woman! This is not the place for giving therapeutic suggestions and recommending the wonders of the inexpensive hormone pills that a woman can take during this period to help ease her over this period. Doctors can do that better.

All I want to say is that though there is a definite change in our physical processes, it comes gradually. While such a major physical change naturally affects our psyche, it does not have to include all those bitchy, witchy characteristics that myths endow it with.

The same is true in the case of a hysterectomy, which is surgical menopause. The need for one can come to any woman at any time, not only in her forties, but in her thirties or even younger. It is a major but usually simple operation.

I was about as stunned as any woman could be at the completely unexpected report from the gynecologist that I needed it. My reaction was like that of someone suddenly confronted with death: One's whole life and certain odd details flash quickly through one's mind. I had never been hospitalized before. I was in a foreign country without any family members near. I even told the doctor that my schedule was too tight to fit in an operation.

The experience turned out to be remarkably positive. In fact, my family, in reply to my reports about some rather hilarious incidents with the doctors and staff, wrote that they didn't think they should have felt so sorry for me after all. But, it wasn't just the funny things that happened before, *during* and after the operation. The experience was positive because it gave me opportunity to face the wonder of physical life from an entirely different perspective, to experience the extraordinary kindness of doctors, staff and friends in that town, to learn to trust the Lord one hundred per cent each minute, to reflect more deeply about the meaning and purpose of existence. I learned so much, and I truly thank God for the experience.

And here I want to underscore again the importance of regular physical exercise. According to the doctor I had an unusually quick recovery. Dr. Chan said it was because my abdominal muscles were strong! So eleven days after surgery I was able to keep my appointment of traveling up the winding mountain roads (keeping my lunch within intact) to begin a month-long leadership camp. (In professional fairness, I should say Dr. Chan gave his consent for me to go at that time only reluctantly.) And though I was obviously not able to do everything the students did and had to conduct workshops while seated, I was not behind schedule, nor did I inconvenience my fellow workers.

I share this personal experience because I want to help relieve the unnecessary fears of some women. If it helps, then God is glorified. And by the way, the gynecologist said before the operation, "You'll feel physically better and emotionally more evenly paced when you no longer have to lose unnecessary blood every month." He was absolutely right.

A Prayer or Two for Growing Older

The older single woman who wrote the following prayer must be a delightful person to know. I enjoy the keen insight and equally keen humor so much that I spontaneously shared them with a good friend. But Adele didn't see anything instructive or funny about the prayer. Then I realized that at twenty-three she had not lived long enough to recognize the middle-age pitfalls which the author depicts with such warm perception!

Lord, Thou knowest better than I know myself that I am growing older, and will someday be old.

Keep me from getting talkative, and particularly from the fatal habit of thinking I must say something on every subject and on every occasion.

Release me from craving to try to straighten out everybody's affairs.

Keep my mind free from the recital of endless details— and give me wings to get to the point.

I ask for grace enough to listen to the tales of others' pains. Help me to endure them with patience.

But seal my lips on my own aches and pains—they are increasing and my love of rehearsing them is becoming sweeter as the years go by.

Teach me the glorious lesson that occasionally it is possible that I may be mistaken.

Keep me reasonably sweet; I do not want to be a saint—some of them are so hard to live with—but a sour old woman is one of the crowning works of the devil.

Make me thoughtful, but not moody; helpful, but not bossy. With my vast store of wisdom, it seems a pity not to use it all. But Thou knowest, Lord, that I want a few friends at the end.

—An Anonymous Mother Superior

And from Dag Hammarskjold, "If only I may grow: firmer, simpler, quieter, warmer."

THE HUMANITY OF JESUS

7

A spate of books about women by women has showered down on us in the last few years. No longer is it necessary for a single woman to write anonymously about her "Honest feelings and intimate thoughts." Nor do her views have to be confined to one chapter buried in the midst of ten chapters of a couple's views of love, courtship and marriage. Study guides about women in the Bible began to be popular before these came. Much of this literature has been stimulating, refreshing and helpful. The trend is generally good and probably overdue.

My intention here is not to have the last word about Jesus and women, how he understood and treated them as full human beings, how Christian male chauvinists need to follow his example and all that. I simply want to take a second look at Jesus Christ himself in the light of all that has been said. I want to review him not only in his relationships with women but with all kinds of other human beings. I want to focus on his human nature.

Defective Views of Jesus' Humanity

From a pagan background I became a Christian as a teenager. Neither at that time nor since then have I had any serious theological problems believing that Jesus of Nazareth is God. My problem was believing that he was as fully *man* as he was fully God. Not that I didn't accept the facts. I knew that Jesus had "voluntarily" laid aside omnipotence, omniscience and omnipresence, and that he could get tired and hungry. I believed in his humanity one hundred per cent— intellectually. But I did not quite make it over that bridge leading to the mainland of practical implications. Certain physical, earthly areas of my life were vaguely blanketed over with Jesus' lordship but not vitally connected with his humanity.

For me God's incarnation in Jesus Christ was only a doctrine necessary for salvation: Jesus had to become a man in order to die physically for our sins. (The beautifully written book of Hebrews is all about this.) But so strong was the teaching of his deity that his humanity became a secondary doctrine. I did not know that our humanity is wonder-ful, not shame-ful. Despite my "understanding" of Hebrews, especially chapter 2, the humanity of Jesus was not real enough for me to see that he *thoroughly* understood *my* humanness.

Later I began to realize how close to heresy this was in virtually ignoring his real humanity.

I think all this was because I grew up spiritually with an incipient evangelical Gnosticism.[4] I was schizophrenic in my thinking and behavior about my body, about sex, about the world, about other material things and certainly about the enjoyment of all these things and related activities.

It would come through like this. One evening in a home Bible study on the temptations of Jesus, a new Christian, lounging on an easy chair in slinky slacks and still slinkier sweater, asked, "Was Jesus ever tempted sexually?" I was the leader and terribly embarrassed, not knowing how to handle the question at all or whether I even wanted to! But some others picked it up, and the discussion that followed proved to be one of the most realistic and helpful ones we ever had. Of course he was, if he was truly human and if Hebrews 4:15-16 is accurate. And if he wasn't and the text is inaccurate, then the incarnation—the whole meaning of Christmas—is one big farce, and we are back to Square One.

When I began meeting more people who both loved Jesus Christ and thoroughly enjoyed God's creation, I was forced to go back to the Gospels for a thorough review of the person of Jesus and a reconsideration of the implications. That was a turning point, a slow but sure turning.

Later on in another country, non-Christians in an evangelistic Bible study confronted me with a question similar to the slinky lady's. This time we were studying Jesus' resurrection appearance to Mary Magdalene. A young Buddhist seeker seriously asked, "Was she Jesus' girl friend?" (This was long before *Jesus Christ Superstar* came on stage.) This time the question was not embarrassing but welcome. For it was a fine opening for presenting the *total* person of Jesus Christ to these students who knew little about him.

But, of course, it is not just this physical aspect of Jesus' humanity that's important, even though it is a telling aspect and even though he himself had some profound things to say on the subject of sex. There are many other eye-opening lessons about him as a complete man without which we cannot understand him as the God-Man.

The Gospel Portrait of Jesus' Humanity

We have already referred to Hebrews as a superb theological statement of Jesus' humanity. But it is essential to return to the historical Jesus Christ in the Gospels. And what do we find there? It is not merely that God appeared on earth. Other religions have similar stories about divine visits to man.

How initially disappointed I was as a young Christian to learn that incarnation stories are not unique to Christianity. For I read in my introductory studies to Hinduism that Vishnu appeared in physical form among men. Then I learned the difference—the vast difference. He only *appeared* as a man. He only *pretended* to be a man. Jesus Christ our God became a real man—no deceptive appearance, no pretense. When Vishnu pushed that monolithic boulder up the hill, he did it with the strength of a god, not a man. But when Jesus resisted the devil's temptations, he did so as a man with a strength from God that is available to all people who ask for God's help.

Jesus was authentically human. This should be his unique appeal to sinners like us. For God is telling us through his perfect Son, "See, here is your human model. This is the kind of person you should be and can be."

His penetrating sense of humor,

his iconoclastic challenges to the establishment,

his devastating calmness in the midst of personal danger,

his compassion and respect for prostitutes as sisters,

his warm magnetism for children,

his redemptive view of crooked politicians,

his unorthodox social habits,

his deep integrity in the face of full-blown dilemmas

—all these characteristics should inspire us to ask, "Who then is this?" The deity of Jesus Christ awes me. So does his humanity.

So far are we from this perfect human model that we cannot appreciate what wholesome humanness is until we see Jesus Christ. Yet so near is he to us now that we need but reach out to touch him. Without him we are troubled, cynical, self-absorbed, bankrupt. With him we are made whole and truly become children of our Father God.

But some may say, "I don't see Christ like this." All I can say here is that you can, if you're willing to toss away the old Sunday school glasses and look again at Jesus of Nazareth in the Gospels—and especially to look at the personal encounters he had with individuals.

These passages continue to be ever increasingly instructive and inspiring for me in life relationships. For instance, I used to think the main point in Luke 7:36-50 was that Jesus was condemning the self-righteousness of Simon the Phari-see and commending the humble love of the forgiven wom-an. These elements are indeed there. But as I've restudied this encounter I've come into a deeper understanding of the mind and heart of Jesus Christ. I observe more closely distinct ways he related to each individual. He did not deal with dif-ferent people by always using the same formula.

Now I see, as elsewhere, that Jesus did not speak and act automatically out of his deity but also procedurally and thoughtfully out of his humanity. On this basis, I've received some fascinating insights, all of which make Jesus more real, more relevant. For instance, Jesus was not primarily con-demning Simon's self-righteousness but encouraging his embryonic faith, step by step. He knew that the Pharisee in him was in conflict for there are several clues about his struggle to believe Jesus. It seems that Jesus heard Simon's silent appeal, "I believe. Help my unbelief!" The conversa-tion between the two was on an intellectual, verbalized level because Simon the Pharisee was an educated person who approached life rationally.

On the other hand, our Lord communicated with the woman non-verbally for she was too emotional for dialogue. She was a person of intuition and action, not logic and ab-straction. Therefore Jesus spoke to her through intuition and action. He not only accepted her by calmly receiving her gifts but clarified and confirmed this to Simon and the others, again by words.

What a man!

What a God!

A Single Woman's Discipleship

With such a Lord, can discipleship be impossible or boring? Hardly! Discipleship for a single woman is not different from discipleship for other Christians. Our life with Christ is nothing if it is not one of constant training as his personal students. Discipleship is not for a select few who are super-spiritual. Not if we understand what Jesus taught about this subject (Lk. 9:23-27, 57-62; 14:25-33). It's for all Christians, or the lordship of Jesus Christ doesn't make sense. That's the way he trains us to live effectively forever.

Each Christian woman must work out her discipleship with fear and trembling in the special circumstances which God has put her in and which he ultimately controls. Marriage is the human context for most women. Singleness is the human context in which I must work out my training program under Christ's leadership and model. My aim should be to please him, whether I'm married or single.

The greater the problems in discipleship, the greater the possibility for growth in character. If the single woman can confront and conquer these problems with God's constant grace, she can become a far more well-rounded human being than a married woman who is complacently satisfied with her status. Why? Because such a married woman may become more and more dependent on her husband, a man who is limited in his wisdom, patience and grace. But the single woman who trusts the Lord takes nothing for granted. She handles problems one at a time with the Lord and his endless resources.

How endless these resources are we can see from John

7:37-38. I don't think many Christians, single or married, really believe Jesus when he said, "If any one thirst, let him come to me and drink." These are simple, monosyllabic words of promise and fulfillment, but profound in significance. Jesus makes *coming to him* and *drinking* the same as *believing in him*. When a person does that, Jesus fully promises, "Out of his heart shall flow rivers of living water." Do you realize what Jesus is saying? He is predicting that in our personal fulfillment we naturally become channels of the Holy Spirit's life-giving refreshment to thirsty ones around us!

Maturity and Rewards

There is nothing inherent in any marital status to make one more spiritual than another. Singleness provides opportunities for growing into a mature person. Marriage provides opportunities for growing into a mature person. One can grow hard and bitter as a single person. One can grow hard and bitter as a married person.

I know sour old maids and sour old marrieds. I know some beautiful marriages that make me wish I could be married like that. But I also know unmarried women and men whose lives are more fulfilled than many married people's. It is not because they are single. I believe it is because by God's grace they are taking their discipleship seriously under Christ's personal tutelage.

They face their problems with reality, often with terrific struggle and always with good humor. They ask the questions, "What can I learn about God through these struggles? What do I learn about my humanity because of this experience? How am I more akin to others because of this new discovery about our common humanity?'' They are strong, beautiful people.

God doesn't intend in the slightest for us singles to live second-rate lives. Neither does he intend that our lives should be lived out simply as dull reflections of some kind of so-called sublimated, compensating life. If we're living life God's way, we're not substituting for marriage. We are living in the very best way that he has lovingly planned for us all along.

Then we will understand, even literally, what Jesus promised his disciples:

Truly, I say to you, there is no one who has left house or brothers or sisters or mother or father or children or lands, for my sake and for the gospel, who will not receive a hundredfold now in this time, houses and brothers and sisters and mothers and children and lands, with persecutions, and in the age to come eternal life. But many that are first will be last, and the last first. (Mk. 10: 29-31)

Notes

[1] A. Bustanaby, "The Pastor and the Other Woman," *Christianity Today*, XVIII, 23 (Aug. 30, 1974).

[2] Paul Tournier, *Learn to Grow Old* (New York: Harper and Row, 1972), p. 101.

[3] Elisabeth Elliot, *Shadow of the Almighty* (New York: Harper, 1958).

[4] Gnosticism was a constant heretical threat to the early church. In the New Testament we see this especially among the Colossian Christians. Innumerable wrong applications were drawn from one wrong belief: Matter is inherently evil. Imagine all the horrible theological and practical implications if this were true! It would mean that creation, the whole world, the physical body, all material things and all physical activities are sinful. Theologically it would mean that man cannot possibly reach God directly. (Gnosticism taught that man's salvation depends on a complicated series of angel intermediaries of which Jesus is but one.) Religious practices would be entirely different from what we follow today (see Col. 2:8-23). It is no wonder Paul vigorously attacked it and in chapter 1 of the letter to the Colossians clearly defines the exalted view of Jesus Christ and the perfection of his works.